From Grain
to Bread

From Grain
to Bread

Ali Mitgutsch

 Carolrhoda Books, Inc., Minneapolis

6|24

First published in the United States of America 1981 by
Carolrhoda Books, Inc. All English language rights reserved.

Original edition © 1971 by Sellier Verlag GmbH, Eching bei München,
West Germany, under the title VOM KORN ZUM BROT.
Revised English text © 1981 by Carolrhoda Books, Inc.
Illustrations © 1971 by Sellier Verlag GmbH.

Manufactured in the United States of America

LIBRARY OF CONGRESS CATALOGING IN PUBLICATION DATA

Mitgutsch, Ali.
   From grain to bread.

      (A Carolrhoda start to finish book)
      Edition for 1971 published under title: Vom Korn
   zum Brot.
      SUMMARY: Highlights the step-by-step process of
   planting wheat seeds, harvesting the crop, grinding
   wheat into flour, and baking bread.

      1. Wheat—Juvenile literature. 2. Bread—Juvenile
   literature. 3. Flour—Juvenile literature. [1. Wheat.
   2. Flour. 3. Bread] I. Title.

   SB191.W5M68413   1981   633.1′1   80-28592
   ISBN 0-87614-155-6

              2   3   4   5   6   7   8   9   10 86 85 84 83 82

From Grain to Bread

Wheat is a kind of grain.

It is used to make many things, including bread.

This farmer is getting ready to plant some wheat.

He puts wheat seeds into the planter behind his tractor.

Then he will drive back and forth over his field.

The seeds will fall from his planter

and be planted in the ground.

With the right amount of rain and sunshine,
wheat plants will grow from the seeds.
First a small green sprout grows out of the ground.
It looks like grass.
Then a head develops at the tip of each plant.
Many **kernels**, or seeds, of grain grow on each head.

As the grain becomes ripe,
it turns from green to gold.
When all the wheat has turned gold,
and the wheat has become hard and dry,
it is ready to be picked, or **harvested**.

The farmer drives a machine called a **combine**
through his wheatfield.
This machine cuts the wheat.
Then it cleans and separates the kernels
from the rest of the plant.
The kernels go into large sacks.
The rest of the plant, called **straw**,
is bundled into bales.
The farmer will save some of the kernels
to plant next year.
He will sell the rest.
He will use the straw as bedding for his horses,
cows, and other animals.

Before the wheat kernels can be used for baking bread,
they must be ground into flour.
This is done by a **miller** at a **flour mill**.
The miller pours the kernels into a large machine.
The machine will grind them into a fine powder.
This miller is grinding white flour
by using only the center of each kernel.
Whole wheat flour is made
by grinding the entire kernel.

Now the flour goes to a bakery.
The baker makes a stiff dough
by mixing it with water and other ingredients.
He shapes this dough into bread, rolls, and pretzels.
Then he puts the dough into the oven to bake.

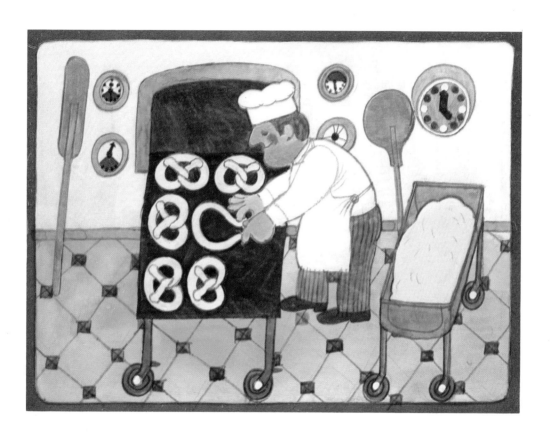

White bread, brown bread, rolls, and cake
are all made from wheat flour.
We can buy them in a bakery.
Or we can buy them in other stores.

This little boy knows how delicious fresh bread tastes.

He has bought a long loaf of bread to take home.

He has also bought a pretzel

so he can eat some fresh, warm bread right away.

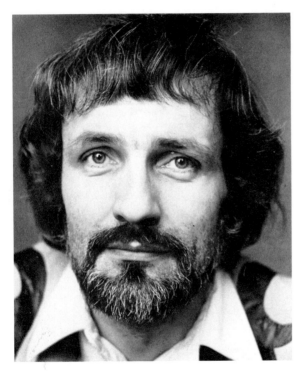

Ali
Mitgutsch

ALI MITGUTSCH is one of Germany's best-known children's book illustrators. He is a devoted world traveler, and many of his book ideas have taken shape during his travels. Perhaps this is why they have such international appeal. Mr. Mitgutsch's books have been published in 22 countries and are enjoyed by thousands of readers around the world.

Ali Mitgutsch lives with his wife and three children in Schwabing, the artists' quarter in Munich. The Mitgutsch family also enjoys spending time on their farm in the Bavarian countryside.

THE CAROLRHODA
START

From Beet to Sugar

From Blossom to Honey

From Cacao Bean to Chocolate

From Cement to Bridge

From Clay to Bricks

From Cotton to Pants

From Cow to Shoe

From Dinosaurs to Fossils

From Egg to Bird

From Egg to Butterfly

From Fruit to Jam

From Grain to Bread

From Grass to Butter

From Ice to Rain

From Milk to Ice Cream

From Oil to Gasoline

From Ore to Spoon

From Sand to Glass

From Seed to Pear

From Sheep to Scarf

From Tree to Table

TO FINISH
BOOKS